Al Sharpton

Al Sharpton

COMMUNITY ACTIVIST

JAY MALLIN

FRANKLIN WATTS
A Division of Scholastic Inc.
New York Toronto London Auckland Sydney
Mexico City New Delhi Hong Kong
Danbury, Connecticut

For Jacob & Jeremy, and their Gramps

All Photographs © 2007: AP/Wide World Photos: 82 (Mike Alexander), 58 (Scott Applewhite), 69 (Ed Bailey), 61 (Diane Bondareff), cover (Jim Bourg), 87 (David Burns), 62 (Mario Cabrera), 77 (Mike Derer), 100 (Damian Dovarganes), 101 (Keith Gedamke/The Item), 50 (Marty Lederhandler), 90 (Andrew Savulich), 89 (Bob Strong), 2 (Susan Walsh), 94 (Emile Wamsteker), 41, 49, 70, 78; Brooklyn College Library Archive: 52; Corbis Images: 72 (Jack Balletti/Bettmann), 84, cover background, 17, 18, 36, 84 (Bettmann), 81 (J.A. Giordano/SABA), 67 (Jon Simon/Bettmann), 38 (Jerry L. Soloway/Bettmann), 21 (Ted Williams), 11 (Francis Wolff/Mosaic Images); Getty Images: 54 (Don Hogan Charles/New York Times Co.), 6, 13 (Ed Clark/Time Life Pictures), 46 (Alfred Eisenstaedt/Pix Inc./Time Life Pictures), 22 (Bill Eppridge/Time Life Pictures), 74 (Jim Estrin/New York Times Co.), 65 (Bill Foley/Time Life Pictures), 24 (Bernard Gotfryd/Hulton Archive), 44 (Declan Haun/Time Life Pictures), 35 (Hulton Archive), 40 (Robert W. Kelley/Time Life Pictures), 27 (David Lees/Time Life Pictures), 42 (Michael Mauney/Time Life Pictures), 14 (New York Times Co./Hulton Archive), 97 (PPO); Jay Mallin Photos: 92; Library of Congress: 26; Magnum Photos/Richard Kalvar: 32; PictureHistory.com: 9; The Image Works/Topham: 30.

Library of Congress Cataloging-in-Publication Data
Mallin, Jay.
  Al Sharpton : community activist / by Jay Mallin.
      p. cm. — (Great life stories)
  Includes bibliographical references and index.
  ISBN-10: 0-531-13872-0 (lib. bdg.)   0-531-17845-5 (pbk.)
  ISBN-13: 978-0-531-13872-4 (lib. bdg.)   978-0-531-17845-4 (pbk.)
  1. Sharpton, Al—Juvenile literature. 2. African Americans—Biography—Juvenile literature. 3. African American clergy—New York (State)—New York—Biography—Juvenile literature. 4. Clergy—New York (State)—New York—Biography—Juvenile literature. 5. Politicians—New York (State)—New York—Biography—Juvenile literature. 6. African American politicians—New York (State)—New York—Biography—Juvenile literature. 7. New York (N.Y.)—Biography—Juvenile literature. I. Title. II. Series.
  E185.97.S54M35 2006
  974.7'100496073092—dc22   2005024622

1 2 3 4 5 6 7 8 9 10 R 16 15 14 13 12 11 10 09 08 07

Contents

These brick row houses are in Brooklyn, New York. The Sharptons owned several brick row houses in Brooklyn, where they lived when Al was born.

A Home in Brooklyn

U p the steps from the sidewalk, in the front door, upstairs, and through the yellow door. This was the way home and one of Alfred Charles Sharpton Jr.'s earliest memories. Through that yellow door was the apartment young Al lived in from his birth on October 3, 1954, until 1960. He shared the apartment with his mother, his father, and his older sister, Cheryl. It wasn't a big apartment. Al had to go through his parents' bedroom to get to the bathroom each morning. But it was comfortable.

Al's parents owned the apartment and the rest of the house, too. Like many in this neighborhood in Brooklyn, New York, the house where Al lived was a brick row house. It was also home to three other families, who paid rent to Al's parents. Like the Sharptons, the other families in the house were African American. Most of the families in the neighboring houses were Italian.

As a child, Al spent a lot of time right around the corner, at a small grocery store and newsstand that his parents also owned. When Al was big enough, he and his sister could walk down the street to the store and play there while their parents worked. They listened as their mom and dad sold groceries or newspapers and chatted with the neighbors.

SOUTHERN ROOTS

Al's parents were both from the South. They had moved north to New York as part of the Great Migration of African Americans from southern farms to northern cities. Al's mom, Ada Richards Sharpton, was born in Alabama. His dad, Alfred Charles Sharpton Sr., was from Florida.

The Great Migration

The Great Migration is the term for a great movement of African Americans from the South to the North. It began in the early decades of the 1900s, when many African Americans who worked on or owned farms in the South began moving to the cities of the North. There were many reasons for the move. Some had to do with hard times for southern cotton farmers and the increase in available jobs in the cities. Escaping racism was a factor, too, although there was racism in the North as well as the South. For many African Americans, the Great Migration led to a whole new way of life in the cities.

Al's dad grew up in a family with seventeen kids. To support the large family, Al's grandfather owned a country store, which was unusual for African Americans in that time and place. When Al was growing up, he used to go with his family to visit his grandparents in Florida. One thing he remembers from that time is that his grandmother was very religious. Although her name was Mamie, her grandchildren called her Big Mama. They used to say, "Big Mama lives at the church."

Al's dad was twenty-nine when Al was born. Al Sr. was handsome and muscular. He'd been a boxer, and he liked to say that he once sparred with boxing champion Sugar Ray Robinson. He was also quite a businessman. Along with the house and the store, he owned two growing contracting companies that poured concrete and renovated buildings. At night he liked taking his family to the

Many African Americans from the South moved to the North during the Great Migration.

famous Apollo Theater in Manhattan's Harlem district to see singers such as Jackie Wilson and James Brown. James Brown would later be very important in young Al's life.

Al's mother, Ada, came from a much smaller family. She was very dignified and slender. She had a sister, Redell. Ada lived with her sister in Brooklyn until she met Al's dad. She, like Al Sr., had been married once before.

Al's father worked several jobs to get ahead. By the time he was thirty-two he owned more than twenty buildings in Brooklyn. Al's mother was very ambitious, too. Her ambitions were focused on her children. She pushed them to do well in school, on their homework, and with whatever activity they did. She taught them that they would succeed. Al was never told "No, you can't do that." He later wrote, "I never knew doubt until I was a grown man."

A NEW CHURCH

Church was important in the life of the Sharptons. Al Sr. and Ada had always gone to Baptist churches. When Al was three, his parents began attending a Pentecostal church. It was called the Washington Temple Church of God in Christ.

The Washington Temple, in Brooklyn's Bedford-Stuyvesant neighborhood, was impressive in every way. The building, formerly a Loew's movie theater, took up a full city block. In front was a huge neon cross that lit up at night. People felt special just to be walking into such a striking building. Inside was a large lobby. Past that was the sanctuary. It had about 2,500 seats downstairs and another 1,000 or so up on the balcony.

Services were held all day Sunday and many weeknights. Presiding over these services was a man who played a key role in Al's life: Bishop Frederick Douglass Washington. Bishop Washington was the son of an Arkansas preacher. As a child, Washington had been a "boy preacher," speaking to his father's congregation when he was as young as age four. That may sound strange, but it was not too unusual in Pentecostal churches. By the time the Sharptons began attending his church, Washington had found great success in Brooklyn. A congregation that had started by meeting in a tent had grown so large that it took over and even filled the old movie theater.

One night, the Sharptons were visiting the Washington Temple when new members were invited to come down to the front and be received into the church. Ada took the hands of Al and Cheryl and marched down with all the others as perhaps two thousand people looked on. It was a

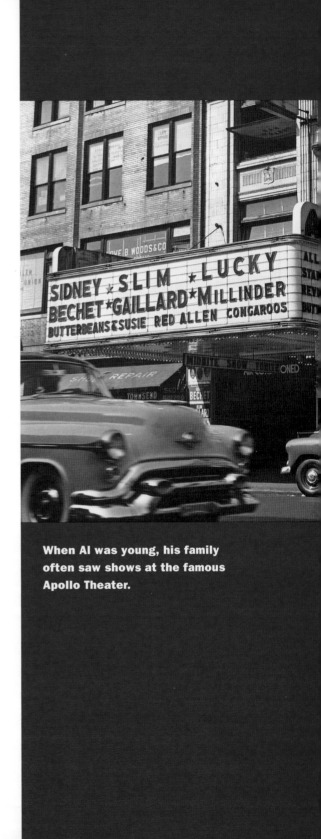

When Al was young, his family often saw shows at the famous Apollo Theater.

completely new experience for Al, who was just three and had spent most of his time in the apartment or his parents' store. He looked up and saw thousands of people singing and clapping. He wasn't afraid. Instead, he was interested in what was going on. One thing that really impressed him was looking up at the enormous pulpit. That's where Bishop Washington and other preachers stood when they spoke to the congregation.

AN UNUSUAL WAY TO PLAY

Spending time in the exciting Washington Temple and listening to the skillful Bishop Washington were bound to affect the young Al Sharpton. At home he started imitating Washington—an unusual way to play, especially for such a young child. When he came home from church, Al would take all his sisters' dolls and line them up in his mother's bedroom. He wasn't interested in playing with the dolls. He wanted to

New York City

The city of New York is one of the world's great cities. It is also the largest city in the United States. The city takes up more than 321 square miles (831 square kilometers) and is home to more than eight million people, which is more people than there are in some states. Because it is so big, the city is divided into five sections called boroughs. They are Brooklyn, the Bronx, Manhattan, Queens, and Staten Island. Manhattan is the business center and home to most of New York's skyscrapers.

preach to them, to speak about Jesus and the Bible, as he'd just watched the bishop do. When he was done preaching to the dolls, Al would put on his mother's wig and pretend to be Washington's wife, Ernestine. She was the church's musical director. Whatever she had sung in the service was what Al would try to sing to the dolls.

Even in other kinds of play, Al would focus on the church. He did play stickball and other games with kids in the neighborhood. But he would also take his blocks and build churches.

At first Al's father didn't like all these church games. But his mother thought they were funny. Besides, she'd always thought that Al would be someone different, someone unusual. Neither of his parents, though, knew that in "playing church," Al was building skills he would use much sooner than they imagined.

While most kids in his neighborhood played outside, Al often practiced preaching.

Al was already an experienced preacher at Washington Temple by the age of seven.

The Boy Preacher

A nice thing about Al's church was that it had something for everyone to do, including the kids. Al and Cheryl became junior ushers at the Washington Temple. They would stand out in the lobby of the church before services and greet people, hand out a weekly bulletin, and escort newcomers to their seats.

One week the woman who organized the junior ushers, Mrs. Hazel Griffin, called the kids together to say the church was planning a special anniversary service. Each of them could take part in it, so she asked them what they wanted to do. One child wanted to read from the Bible during the service. Another wanted to sing. Then Mrs. Griffin looked at Al and asked him what he wanted to do.

"I want to preach!" the four-year-old blurted out. The other kids thought that was a strange job for a kid, especially such a young one. They laughed at him. But it made sense to Al, who had been pretending to preach to the dolls at home for months. It made sense to Mrs. Griffin, too, because she knew that Bishop Washington himself had given sermons in his own father's church when he was only four.

So Mrs. Griffin talked to the bishop. They agreed that young Al could indeed preach to the whole congregation on the special anniversary, July 9, 1959. Al had an older half-sister and half-brother, Ernestine and Thomas, both from his mom's first marriage. They helped him think of what to say and helped him practice.

When the day came, they put a box for Al to stand on behind the offering table. That way, people would be able to see him. Bishop Washington, who would become Al's first mentor, encouraged him as he got ready. Al put on a gold robe, climbed up on the box, and started his

Mentors

Most of us learn from all types of people: our teachers, our parents, our friends. Many people, from children to grown-ups, also have a special relationship with an older friend who helps them make decisions about important issues such as a new school or a new job. This kind of friend is sometimes called a mentor. Some schools have mentoring programs in which adults or older kids help younger ones. Even people who work as executives at big companies often look for mentors. Al had a series of mentors throughout his life, including Reverend Adam Clayton Powell Jr., Bishop Frederick Douglass Washington, Reverend Jesse Jackson, and James Brown.

sermon. There were about nine hundred people in the audience, and they were all looking at him. He was nervous at first. But once he began, the audience started joining in by saying "Amen," which they did to encourage preachers. They stood and swayed and clapped. Soon Al felt right at home.

Al and his sermon were a great success. Even better was what happened afterward. Washington said that if Al wanted to be a preacher, he couldn't preach just once. He would have to do it regularly. So they agreed that Al would give a sermon once a month. This would change the young boy's life forever.

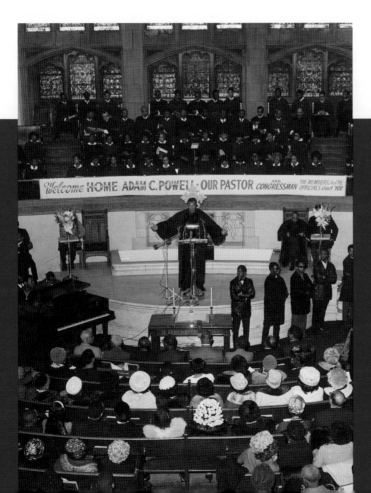

One of Al Sharpton's mentors, Reverend Adam Clayton Powell Jr., was a charismatic preacher who became a representative in the U.S. Congress.

Pentecostal churches are known for their lively services. Al traveled to many churches as a child and became a popular preacher.

THE WONDERBOY PREACHER

There were some good sides and some bad sides to being a boy preacher. One good side was that Al's father, who hadn't liked him preaching to dolls, became very proud of him. As Al preached each month, he became better and better at it. People outside the Washington Temple heard of him and invited him to speak at their churches. Al's dad would drive him all over New York State so other churches could hear the child they were calling the Wonderboy. By the time Al was nine, he even traveled around the country with Bishop Washington.

On the other hand, as a child, it was strange to be known as a preacher. One difficulty came when Al began first grade at Public School 134. His teacher would always have the students write their names on their schoolwork. But instead of writing something like "Alfred Sharpton Jr.," he would write "Minister Alfred Sharpton" or "Reverend Alfred Sharpton." His surprised teacher didn't believe this was the correct way for students to write their names. The teacher sent for Al's mom. She tried to explain that her son was indeed a sort of minister. "Not in school, he's not," answered the teacher, who still didn't like the idea.

Some of the other children felt uncomfortable around Al, too. Even though he played games with the kids at school and in his neighborhood, they always knew he was different. The same boy they were playing stickball with was the kid their parents went to church to hear. After the services, instead of running around the halls with the other kids or trying to sneak extra cake and punch, Al would go up and sit in Washington's office. The bishop was always up there reading books and writing. So Al would sit and read books and write, too. When the bishop underlined what he was reading, Al would underline what was in his own book, even when he didn't understand it.

A NEW HOME

As Al was learning to be a preacher, his father was doing better in business. Al Sr. was able to buy more and more buildings, where he rented apartments to people. His contracting businesses were growing, too.

Eventually these businesses did so well that the Sharptons moved to a new home. It was in a nice neighborhood in Queens. It had ten rooms, a finished basement, and a lawn. Al used to read in the basement and he built himself a make-believe church there. At one point, Al's father was doing so well that he bought new cars every year for himself and his wife. The family still went to the Washington Temple for church in their old neighborhood, but the Sharpton kids went to school in the new neighborhood. Al's parents thought this school was better.

New York World's Fair

More than fifty-one million people visited the New York World's Fair from the time it opened in 1964 until it closed in 1965. The rides and exhibits were designed to show people what life would be like in the future with computers and space travel. Exhibits featured the latest advances in electricity, chemistry, and other fields. At the center of the fair was a stainless-steel model of the Earth, twelve stories high and circled by the tracks of three satellites.

About four years later, in 1964, the great New York World's Fair was held in Queens. This was the largest world's fair ever held in the United States. It took up almost 1 square mile (2.6 square kilometers) with its pavilions, exhibits, and rides. One day the gospel singer Mahalia Jackson was asked to sing at the fair. She invited the young reverend, whom she knew from the Washington Temple, to preach a short sermon between her sets while she took a break. Al, who was only ten, looked out on thousands of people as he spoke that day. He later wrote that he was never even scared, "because my mother had told me that I could do it." Later his connection with Mahalia Jackson led to his going on tour with her as far away as Seattle, Washington.

When Al was ten, he was ordained a minister in the Pentecostal Church, making him a "reverend" for real. Bishop Washington named him junior pastor. From then until he was eighteen, the boy preacher would lead Friday night services at the Washington Temple.

But just before he was ordained, a dark cloud came over Al's life. His father moved out of the comfortable house and left the family in Queens. Soon the rest of the Sharptons would have to find another place to live as well.

Mahalia Jackson was an acclaimed gospel singer whose father was a preacher.

On November 9, 1965, there was a massive power outage that left New York City dark for more than five hours.

THREE

On Their Own

Al was just nine and a half years old when his mother came and woke him with terrible news. His father had moved out, along with Al's stepsister. In the months to come Al's parents would be getting a divorce.

This breakup of the family was awful news in itself. Just as bad was the fact that, without Al Sr., the rest of the Sharptons had no money. Although Ada Sharpton used to work, she had given it up to be a full-time mom.

With no money, there was no way to pay the bills. Their car, which they were still paying for, was taken away. Then the gas and electricity were cut off. There they were, living in a big, fancy house with no heat or electricity. The other kids made fun of Al because he did his homework by candlelight. Their teasing ended, though, one night in 1965 when there was a big blackout in New York City and everybody's electricity went off. Those same neighbors who had teased Al had to come over to the Sharpton house to borrow some candles for themselves!

As part of the changes in the family, the Sharptons had to go to court. Their case was handled by a judge who'd never heard of the idea

After his parents' divorce, Al moved back to Brooklyn where children played on pavement instead of lawns.

of a boy preacher. This judge was worried that Al was being forced to preach against his will so his family would have money. The judge called Al into his private office to speak with him. "I order you not to preach anymore," said the judge. "Do you understand?"

The young reverend said he understood. The next Friday, Al was to preach at Washington Temple, as he did every week. He went in and stood behind the big pulpit where no one could see him. He was afraid to get in trouble, afraid there might even be police watching. But when it was time for him to stand up and give the sermon, Al did so. There were no court officials checking up on him.

Two weeks later, Al and his family were back in court. The judge asked him if he had done any preaching. Al answered honestly that he had, despite the judge's orders. The judge asked him why. Did someone make him? No, he told the judge, he did it "because I believe in what I'm doing." The judge, surprised, said Al could continue doing what he believed in.

MOVING BACK

At first, Al's mother took the change in the family very hard. She even checked into a hospital for a time because she was so distressed. But Ada Sharpton was a strong woman. She was determined that she and her children would be all right.

Ada signed herself and her children up for welfare. She realized they would not be able to afford the house in Queens, so she moved the family back to Brooklyn. At first they lived with a friend from Washington Temple whose home was in the housing projects. It was quite a change

The Projects

During the Great Depression of the 1930s, when poor people started living in tent cities, President Franklin Delano Roosevelt and others became concerned. The government tried to help people live in better, more sanitary conditions by building housing projects (below). Working people could afford to live there. Eventually, these projects became dangerous places, full of crime and drugs. But the Reverend Al Sharpton Jr. remembers that, when he lived there, gangs were limited and honest people were safe.

from the house with a lawn in Queens. In the projects, people were stacked on top of one another in apartments. And the only "yard" was the basketball court, which was always full of kids.

Despite moving back to Brooklyn, Al continued to go to his school in Queens, PS 134. He spent hours on the subway to get there. Though he was very bright, Al had trouble concentrating on schoolwork. He was worried about his mom and upset about his dad. He found he couldn't sit in class. Sometimes he would even wander the halls. Al could have gotten in trouble if it weren't for two teachers who understood what he

Al spent many weekend afternoons at Brentano's bookstore.

was going through. Mr. and Mrs. Greenberg would talk with the unhappy young boy and listen to his worries and troubles.

Other people helped, too. The Reverend Walter Banks, another preacher at Washington Temple, would pick up Al every weekend and take him into Manhattan. Banks wanted Al to learn about religious traditions outside Washington Temple. He would take the young reverend to famous places of worship, such as the Roman Catholic Saint Patrick's Cathedral or the Dutch Reformed Church's Marble Collegiate Church, with a congregation that has been holding services for more than three hundred years.

Then the two would head for Brentano's bookstore on Fifth Avenue. Al would pick out books, books, and more books, and Banks would pay for them. Later, Banks would quiz his young friend to make sure he was actually reading all those books. Perhaps to his surprise, he would find that Al was doing so. Al believes his love of reading traces back to those days he spent browsing for books with Reverend Banks.

One day, when Al was browsing in a bookstore, he came upon a book whose cover showed a picture of a minister wearing a clergyman's collar. Al was excited, since he was a minister himself. He learned that the man's name was Adam Clayton Powell Jr. Not only was Powell a famous African American minister, he was also a powerful congressman from New York. The book cost ninety-nine cents. Al bought it with his own money.

WHO'S AT THE DOOR?

After reading about the Reverend Powell the young preacher wanted to learn about other famous African Americans. He had actually met some of these people, including the Reverend Martin Luther King Jr., at

Washington Temple. But it wasn't until his parents' divorce and all the upheaval it caused in his life that Al really began to pay attention to civil rights leaders like Dr. King.

Perhaps his new awareness had to do the with the moves he'd made—first to the fancy house in Queens, then into the housing projects in Brooklyn. Up until he'd lived in the projects, Al had always lived in homes his parents owned. His parents had always been their own bosses, at the old grocery store and newsstand and in his father's real estate and construction businesses. This was not the experience of most African Americans, especially those who were now Al's neighbors. But unlike his new neighbors, Al knew that a better life was possible. He had lived it himself.

Marcus Garvey

Marcus Garvey was a publisher, businessman, and speaker. Born in Jamaica in 1887, he traveled widely before coming to the United States. There he went on a lecture tour to promote his organization, the Universal Negro Improvement Association. He urged African Americans to be proud of their race. Garvey also fostered black nationalism, which at times included a "back-to-Africa" movement and the idea of a separate nation for blacks. Garvey was deported back to Jamaica in 1927, but he continued to work for black nationalism. In 1928, he presented a "Petition of the Negro Race" to the League of Nations. (The League of Nations was an international organization that preceded the United Nations.) Marcus Garvey died in 1940.

Despite the family difficulties he faced, the young reverend's career as a preacher continued to grow. He traveled beyond New York, around the country, and to the Caribbean islands, too. Sometimes he toured with entertainers, such as his gospel-singer friend Mahalia Jackson. When Al was just ten, Bishop Washington took about a dozen people from the church, including Al, on a three-week tour of the Caribbean. They went to Haiti, Jamaica, Barbados, Trinidad, and Puerto Rico, preaching and

Marcus Garvey promoted black nationalism through his lectures, tours, and publications.

holding services along the way. Al wanted to see what those places were like beyond the churches. Sometimes he would go exploring with the bishop's daughter, Frederica. She was just one year older than he was.

The kids' expeditions usually didn't get very far—except when the tour arrived in Kingston, Jamaica. While reading about Adam Clayton Powell, Al had begun to learn about Marcus Garvey, a black nationalist who had been born in Jamaica. Al knew Garvey was dead, but he thought it would be interesting to meet Garvey's family. To his wonder, Amy Jacques Garvey, Marcus's widow, was listed in the phone book. Al called her and introduced himself as the Reverend Alfred Sharpton Jr. from the United States. He said he had read a lot about Mr. Garvey. So Mrs. Garvey invited him to come over the next day.

That morning Al got up, put on his Sunday best, and climbed into a cab. He asked for 12 Mona Road. When he got to the home he knocked on the door. Mrs. Garvey came and looked out the peephole on the door. She didn't see anyone. Al was standing there, but he was way too short to be seen. So she didn't answer the door. Al knocked again, and they repeated this three times. Finally, Mrs. Garvey opened the door and saw Al. At first, she was angry. She thought he'd been playing a prank on her. Then she started laughing. She realized that this boy, all dressed up, was the preacher from America she had been expecting.

Al spent most of the day with her, having tea and listening to her answers as he asked every question he could think of about Marcus Garvey. After Al left Jamaica, he stayed in touch with Mrs. Garvey. The two new friends wrote to each other two or three times a year.

By the mid-1960s, the civil rights movement had gained momentum across the nation, including New York.

The Activist

Al eventually transferred from his old school in Queens to Somers Junior High, JHS 252, in Brooklyn. His mother had been able to move her family out of the projects after a few months. They ended up in a five-bedroom apartment in Brooklyn's East Flatbush neighborhood.

Now Al's mom was working as a domestic servant in Manhattan's Greenwich Village. The changes in her family life did not dampen her ambitions for her children, though. Each day, Al walked her to the subway as she went to work. She would lecture him about how he could achieve anything he wanted in his life.

Al was becoming increasingly interested in politics and social justice. Partly, this came from the changes he had seen in his own life. And partly, it reflected the mood of the country at the time and the predicament of African Americans in particular. The year Al Sharpton was born, 1954, was also the year the Supreme Court made its famous ruling in *Brown v. Board of Education*. That court said that requiring African American and white children to attend separate schools, a system called segregation, violated the U.S. Constitution.

The *Brown* decision was a turning point in the fight against discrimination. But this was only the beginning of the battle, not the end. Discrimination in New York City, where Al lived, was less obvious than the discrimination that prompted the *Brown* decision. However, back when Al's father was taking the family to visit their grandparents in Florida, the young reverend had seen a more open example of discrimination.

One day, on one of these trips, Al's father stopped the car at a hamburger joint in North Carolina. He got out to buy some food for his family. The people at the hamburger stand said they didn't serve African

A Topeka Third-Grader

The case of *Brown v. Board of Education* was filed in 1951 on behalf of a third-grade girl, Linda Brown, who was forced to walk a mile every day to a school that was just for African Americans. She had to do this even though she lived just a few blocks from another school reserved for whites. At first, the courts said it was perfectly acceptable to send African Americans and whites to separate schools. But on May 17, 1954, all nine members of the U.S. Supreme Court agreed that having separate schools for blacks and whites was "inherently unequal." It was against the law. It took years to put their decision into effect.

Americans. They also used an unacceptable word for "African American." Al couldn't believe that his dad took the abuse and just got back into the car. Up to that point, he didn't know anyone could tell his father "no" like that. His father tried to explain, but it wasn't until the reverend was much older that he understood. There in the South, with his wife and children in the car and no friends for hundreds of miles, his dad had good reason not to create a fuss.

By junior high young Al was much more political and much more aware of what was going on around the country. The civil rights movement was in full swing. Congress had extended the *Brown* decision with laws such as the Civil Rights Act of 1964 and the Voting Rights Act of 1965. These laws prohibited discrimination in voter registration and in hiring, as well as in public places and in programs paid for by the federal government.

The people in Al's Pentecostal church tended to avoid politics, but Al

Before the civil rights movement, many southern businesses wouldn't serve African Americans.

and his friends didn't. In junior high his best friends were a white boy named Richard Farkas and an African American boy named Dennis Neal. The three friends were so interested in politics that they nicknamed themselves after political figures. Dennis liked to call himself Stokely Carmichael, after a leader of the Student Nonviolent Coordinating Committee and the Black Panther Party. Richard liked to be known as Bobby Kennedy. This politician was the brother of

Stokely Carmichael was an important figure in the civil rights movement. He continued his political activism throughout his life.

President John F. Kennedy. Al used the nickname Adam, after Adam Clayton Powell Jr., the minister and congressman whose book had attracted his attention a few years earlier.

EVERYBODY KNOWS YOU

By this point, the young reverend knew about Powell from more than just reading about him. Powell was famous in New York and across the country as one of only two African Americans in the U.S. Congress. Al wanted to meet him.

Powell's church was in Manhattan's Harlem neighborhood, which Al's mother thought was not safe to visit. Still, Al managed to convince her to let him go there with his sister, Cheryl. One Sunday, they

Adam Clayton Powell Jr.

Adam Clayton Powell Jr., like his father, was a Baptist minister and pastor of the Abyssinian Baptist Church in New York City. He organized public campaigns to force employers to treat African American employees better. At one point he even targeted employers at the 1939 World's Fair. In 1944, he was elected to Congress. He was the first African American to become a committee chairman in the U.S. House of Representatives, heading its powerful Education and Labor Committee. Powell oversaw the passage of many important laws in the 1960s. But his political career ended in scandal after he abused his power by taking committee funds for his own use.

Adam Clayton Powell Jr. was a member of Congress for more than twenty years. His ability to affect political and social change inspired Sharpton.

attended a service at Powell's church, the Abyssinian Baptist Church. But Powell wasn't there that Sunday. Al was struck by how quiet and refined the service was, compared to the services at the Washington Temple. Because Powell hadn't been there, Al kept asking his mother to let him go again. She finally agreed a few weeks later.

This time, partway through the service, Adam Clayton Powell himself came out of a side door. He was tall and handsome. He strode to the pulpit and preached a sermon on the theme "God is love." The congregation, which had seemed so refined and proper on Al's previous visit, came alive, shouting "Amen!" and clapping their hands.

After the service Al found his way to Powell's office. There he told the church secretary that "the Reverend Alfred Sharpton" wanted to meet with the Reverend Powell. She looked down at this young boy and laughed, leaving him standing there in the hallway. Al waited ten minutes. Then he called her back and asked again. She finally agreed to at least ask the great minister and congressman if Al could come in. The secretary reappeared just a few minutes later and sheepishly asked Al to follow her.

She led Al to Powell's office. The famous minister stood in the middle of the room, wearing pants but no shirt as he changed out of clothes that had become sweaty while he was preaching. Powell looked at Al and said, "Here's the 'Wonderboy Preacher' from my good friend F. D. Washington's church, Alfred Sharpton." Al was in heaven—his hero, Adam Clayton Powell, knew who he was! "I listen to Bishop Washington's broadcast when I'm in town," Powell told the young reverend. "Everybody knows you."

To Al's delight and amazement, Powell invited him to a nearby hangout for a soda. There Al listened in wonder as Powell talked with people from every walk of life, from poor workers to famous sports celebrities. They all wanted to speak with Powell. After that amazing afternoon, the young reverend went to visit Powell every chance he got, spending time with the minister as he listened to people and tried to help them out.

Later, when Al was twelve and Powell got into trouble in his political career, the congressman's young friend formed the Youth Committee for Powell. The members collected signatures on a petition that supported Powell. It was perhaps the young reverend's first experience as a political activist.

MOVED BY A SONG

With the civil rights movement sweeping the country, Al wanted to become involved. A central figure in the movement was the Reverend Dr. Martin Luther King Jr., the leader of the Southern Christian

Leadership Conference (SCLC). The SCLC had set up a program called Operation Breadbasket. This program used public campaigns, boycotts (refusals to do business with a company), and other economic pressures to convince employers to hire and promote African Americans. In many ways, Operation Breadbasket was similar to campaigns run by Adam Clayton Powell thirty years earlier.

In Brooklyn, Operation Breadbasket was headed by a minister named William Jones. Al went to meet with Jones and then went to some of Operation Breadbasket's meetings. He even tried to get other kids to go, too. But the meetings seemed kind of boring to Al, and besides, he was involved in other issues at the time.

Then on the night of April 4, 1968, while Al and his family were

Martin Luther King Jr. (center) helped organize and participated in the March on Washington for Jobs and Freedom. More than 250,000 demonstrators joined him on August 28, 1963.

watching a TV show called *Ironsides*, there was an announcement that Dr. King had been shot in Memphis, Tennessee. Al's mother started crying. Al admired Dr. King and had even met him. But he didn't understand why his mother was crying so hard. She acted as if the civil rights leader had been a member of their own family. She told her son that if he had grown up as she had in Alabama, facing discrimination every time he rode a bus or went to school or even needed a bathroom, then he would understand why she was so upset.

Some months after Dr. King was assassinated, a movie came out about the civil rights leader. In the movie there was a song that asked, "What will happen, now that the King of Love is dead?" The young reverend heard that song as a challenge to himself. He felt like he wasn't doing enough. He had somehow let Dr. King down. So Al went back to Operation Breadbasket and asked if he could organize a youth division.

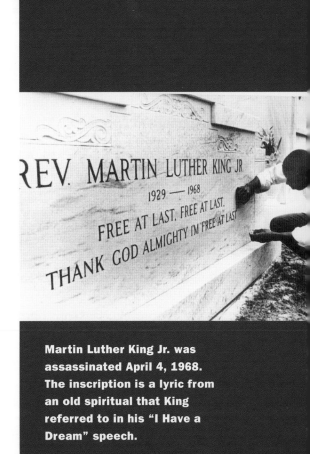

Martin Luther King Jr. was assassinated April 4, 1968. The inscription is a lyric from an old spiritual that King referred to in his "I Have a Dream" speech.

A few months later, Operation Breadbasket opened a new office. The program's national director came to town for the ribbon-cutting ceremony. He was a young, up-and-coming activist named Jesse Jackson. "Reverend Jesse," as everyone called him, didn't seem to really notice the program's youth director when they were introduced. But then the singer Mahalia Jackson showed up. She had met Reverend Jesse in Chicago. She arranged for Al to speak to the crowd, and she broke the ice between Al and Reverend Jesse.

In Jesse Jackson, Al had a new hero. He even changed his appearance to look more like Jackson. Though Al had once favored suits and ties and crew cuts, he now chose an Afro hairstyle and long sideburns and started wearing vests. He even went to Greenwich Village to buy a big, gold medallion to wear on a chain, just like Jesse Jackson did. In 1969, Jackson appointed the fourteen-year-old as Operation Breadbasket's youth director.

Al's first Operation Breadbasket campaign was directed against a clothing store named Robert Hall. Its customers were mainly African Americans. But the store did not include African Americans among its top executives or the business owners it worked with. With Al managing

Jesse Jackson was the national director of Operation Breadbasket.

the youth, Operation Breadbasket called for a boycott of the store. The group demanded contracts for African American businesses, summer jobs for inner-city kids, and training programs so workers could move up in the company. The store was forced to cooperate.

An even bigger battle involved the schools, including Tilden High School where Al would soon be enrolling. Members of the local African American communities wanted local school boards to control the schools. The teachers' union was opposed to the idea. Leaders of the black communities called a strike, saying they would close the schools by keeping their kids home unless their side won out. Al and his friends marched with signs outside the schools as that dispute continued.

At Tilden, Al joined the debating team and the Afro-American Club and worked on the school newspaper. By his second year he was president of the Afro-American Club, which met almost daily at his home. Al was also head of a group called the Martin Luther King Memorial Committee. This club got permission to hang up a portrait of Dr. King and a plaque about him at the school. It was the first school in the city to do so.

Al joined students from several ethnic groups who visited different schools to promote racial harmony. Things were anything but harmonious at Al's school, though. With the experience of the school strike and the mood sweeping the country, the students would call a strike for just about anything—even bad cafeteria food! Al was one of the ringleaders of these strikes. For an experienced activist like Al, calling a boycott and shutting down the school was a piece of cake. He later told people the principal would call his mom in the morning and ask, "How's Alfred doing this morning? I need to know how many problems we're going to have at school today!"

Singer Harry Belafonte participates in an Operation Breadbasket rally.

FIVE

A Protest at the A & P

Working for Operation Breadbasket, Al held meetings for young people every Wednesday night at the Reverend Jones's church. Al had them put up flyers to recruit more youth at every church whose ministers were involved in Operation Breadbasket. Soon he had built up an "army" of about five hundred young people who could be counted on to turn out for protests and other actions.

Al was involved in successful campaigns against about fifteen companies. Of all the actions Al organized during his time with Operation Breadbasket, the biggest was against a grocery store chain in 1971. It was the A & P, which had stores everywhere in the New York area and across the country. The people at Operation Breadbasket were unhappy that the stores didn't often hire people from local neighborhoods. They also

thought the chain put lower-quality food in its inner-city stores and did not keep those stores as clean as stores in nicer neighborhoods.

The young reverend's youth division and other adult members of Operation Breadbasket tried picketing A & P stores in the area. They would shout "Boycott A & P" or "Unfair Practices" at people heading into the stores, to let them know what was going on. But people didn't seem to care enough. Al even remembers one lady who got so angry she ran a shopping cart into him.

The next step for Al and other Operation Breadbasket leaders was to try to meet with the executives of A & P. William J. Kane, the president of A & P, refused to see them. He also refused to meet with Jesse Jackson and another national civil rights leader, Ralph Abernathy. So the Reverend Jones decided to try another tactic. He called for a sit-in, right in Kane's offices.

One day, around 6 P.M., Jones, Al, and more than thirty other ministers went to the A & P national headquarters at 420

Tactics for Change

People who are unhappy with a government or business have developed special ways to make their concerns known. One tactic is the picket line, in which people carry signs and walk back and forth outside an office or business. Another is the boycott, in which people agree not to shop at certain stores or buy certain goods until changes are made. A third is the protest or demonstration, where a large group carries signs, gives speeches, and marches through town. Al Sharpton and other civil rights leaders used these tactics as well as others.

Lexington Avenue in Manhattan. They walked in, strode past the secretary outside Kane's office, and went right into the office. Kane wasn't there. So the group said they wouldn't leave until they could meet with him. The A & P staff called the police. Al and the other ministers just sat there singing "We Shall Overcome" and other protest and religious songs.

"I'M SITTING AT YOUR DESK"

By 9 P.M., it was clear the A & P staff had decided not to have the police arrest the protesters. But they weren't going to let the group meet with William Kane either. So the ministers began to get comfortable for an all-night stay.

Al, the youngest of the group, had an idea. He picked up the phone on Kane's desk and dialed directory assistance. He asked for Kane's home phone number, and the operator gave it to him. So Al called it.

"Mr. Kane?" he asked when a man answered the phone. "Yes," replied the voice. "My name is Reverend Alfred Sharpton," Al told the A & P president. "I'm a young minister, and right this minute I'm sitting at your desk. I want to know why you won't meet with Reverend Jones and Operation Breadbasket and other leaders of our community." William Kane was furious. He shouted at Al over the phone. He tried to lecture Al about proper respect for other people's property. But Al just kept responding with his group's positions on fairness and giving something back to the community. Finally, Kane just hung up. Meanwhile, the older ministers in the room were laughing. They couldn't believe the young reverend had actually called him at home.

During that night in the office a white security guard came and asked Al if he'd had anything to eat. Al said he hadn't but that he didn't want to go out. The guard offered to help. He went and got Al a couple of hamburgers. "I respect you men and what you're doing," the guard said. "I hope my grandchildren believe in something like you do one day."

By the next afternoon, the ministers were still sitting in Kane's office. Newspaper and TV reporters had come to write about and broadcast news of the sit-in. So A & P officials decided to ask the police to arrest the ministers. Reverend Jones and the others gathered around the reception desk to wait for the police. Al was ready to be arrested, too. Then he saw the security guard he'd met the night before. The guard asked the police not to arrest "the kid." The other ministers agreed that Al shouldn't be arrested. They were afraid it could be used against them if it appeared they'd encouraged Al, a juvenile, to break the law. So Al went and stood by his friend the guard as the others were arrested and taken off by police.

Al wanted to be close at hand, though. He went to the jail and called his mom to say that he would be spending the night there. Then he lay down to sleep. At about two o'clock in the morning, someone woke him up and said he had an important phone call. Al went to the phone and answered. "Young buck, give me a report, tell me what happened," the voice on the phone said. It was the Reverend Jesse Jackson. Al practically jumped for joy. It was the first time Jesse Jackson had ever called him. Al gave the national director of Operation Breadbasket a full report. Then Jackson asked Al to call together the youth and some ministers—at least those who weren't in jail—for a rally the next day. Jackson said he was flying in to New York immediately. He told Al, "We're going back to A & P!"

William J. Kane, the president of A & P, refused to speak to the protestors in his office and had them arrested.

HELP FROM CHICAGO

Jesse Jackson had good reason to be concerned about A & P. The grocery chain had forty stores in inner-city areas of Chicago, where Jackson was based. When Jackson arrived in New York, a whole new Operation Breadbasket team, including young people from Al's youth division, returned to 420 Lexington Avenue. A & P employees turned off the elevators to stop the group from getting to the executive offices. So Jackson

Jesse Jackson and eleven others from Operation Breadbasket were arrested during a sit-in at the A & P offices in New York City on February 2, 1971.

Blood on His Sweater

The Reverend Jesse Jackson, a young aide to Dr. Martin Luther King, first came to national attention when Dr. King was shot and killed in Memphis on April 4, 1968. Jackson had been standing right next to Dr. King at the time. The next day, Jackson appeared at a rally in Chicago wearing the sweater he said had been stained by Dr. King's blood. Jackson soon became a leader in his own right, forming two national groups and even running for president.

asked Al to call in TV and newspaper reporters. When they came, Jackson led them to the grounded elevators and sat down inside one.

This time, the police moved in more quickly and started arresting people. But they refused to arrest Al and the other young people. They did arrest Jackson, though. He and eleven others walked out of the lobby into police vans. That made the news the next day. Now A & P executives saw how much negative attention they were getting, and they realized that Operation Breadbasket wasn't about to give up. They finally agreed to meet and negotiate with the protesters.

In the end, the company's executives promised to guarantee hundreds of new jobs for African Americans. They also promised that their stores would carry products made by African American companies and that A & P would use black-owned businesses, from banks to janitorial services. After that, store executives met monthly with members of Operation Breadbasket to make sure the agreement was followed and strengthened. It was Operation Breadbasket's most important victory up to that point.

After graduating from Tilden High School, Al attended Brooklyn College.

SIX

The Godfather of Soul

In the spring of 1972, Al Sharpton went onstage at Tilden High School to receive his diploma and graduate. He also received the school's Community Service Award. It was handed to him by the same principal who used to call his mother to find out if the "troublemaker" was going to cause any problems that day. "I never in all my years as principal have been so glad to give a student his diploma!" said the principal. Everyone laughed.

The occasion was not as happy for Al as it might have been. He was sad because his father wasn't there. Al had neither seen nor heard from his dad in years. But Al's mother told him she didn't want to see him unhappy. She felt she had worked too hard for that. "Boy, I scrubbed floors to see you graduate high school and get you accepted to Brooklyn

College. When they call your name and you walk across that stage, if you don't smile for nobody but me, you smile, because I fought to see this day." So Al smiled at his mom when he walked across the stage.

Al was the first in his family to graduate from high school. He was also the first to go to college. However, college did not go well. Later, he said he believed he'd made a mistake in deciding to study contemporary politics. The problem was that the young man felt he already knew the subject well, maybe even better than his teachers. If they taught about the civil rights movement and Dr. King and his widow, Coretta Scott

U.S. Representative Shirley Chisholm of Brooklyn was a passionate civil rights leader.

King, or if they taught about national politics and Adam Clayton Powell and African American congresswoman Shirley Chisholm—well, Al knew those people. He had worked with them himself, and he didn't think his teachers had much to add.

At Brooklyn College, Al was involved in the Black Student Union and, just as in high school, the debate team. He continued to read, just as he had when the Reverend Banks from the Washington Temple was buying him books. Once he saw Jesse Jackson reading a book by Paul Tillich, a famous theologian, or religious scholar. So the young reverend went out and bought all of Tillich's books. Jackson also encouraged Al to stay in school.

But it didn't work. In what he later concluded was a mistake, Al dropped out after two years at the college.

A GROUP OF HIS OWN

In 1971, while he was still in high school, Al Sharpton had to make a very difficult decision. Jesse Jackson split from the Southern Christian Leadership Conference, which Dr. King had led, and from its Operation Breadbasket program. Jackson then started his own group, People United to Save Humanity, or PUSH. (Later, the organization's name was changed to People United to Serve Humanity.) Most of the people involved in Operation Breadbasket went with Jackson. But the Reverend Jones, Sharpton's friend, stayed with the SCLC.

That left Al with a difficult decision. Both Jones and Jackson were his role models and teachers. Now, like many people in the civil rights movement, he had to choose sides. In the end, he left Operation

Breadbasket, though he always stayed friends with Jones. However, rather than join PUSH, Al decided it was time to start his own group.

He went to Bayard Rustin, a civil rights activist who had worked with Dr. King to set up the SCLC. Al told Rustin he wanted to start a new group of his own, using his friends from Tilden High School and from Operation Breadbasket. It would be called the National Youth Movement (NYM). Rustin gave him $500 to help him get started.

To make the new group official, Al needed to incorporate it. That would give it a special status, like a big company or an important nonprofit group. This was a problem for Al. At age seventeen he was legally too young to do such a thing. He needed to hire a lawyer to handle the incorporation, and that would cost $3,000. So he turned to successful businesspeople he knew from Operation Breadbasket, and they helped in a number of ways. Al was able to hold a fund-raising luncheon at the

Soul Brother Number One

James Brown—singer, dancer, and bandleader—is one of the most important music figures of the twentieth century. As a teenager he was convicted of armed robbery, and he worked as a boxer and a baseball player before turning to music. His band toured the country and was only moderately successful until 1963. That's when a live performance by Brown and his band at New York's Apollo Theater was released on a record. It made him nationally famous. He is credited with inventing the style known as funk. Rock, jazz, and hip-hop artists say they've learned and borrowed from Brown's recordings.

New York Hilton in 1972. People paid to attend the luncheon and hear speakers, such as Congresswoman Shirley Chisholm. Using the money he raised, Al hired a lawyer named David Dinkins to do the legal work. Years later, Dinkins became mayor of New York City.

A FAMOUS SUPPORTER

Even after the National Youth Movement was incorporated, Al had to keep raising money for its operations. He was working on this in 1973 when he heard from a radio station disc jockey he knew. The disc jockey said he'd gotten a call from no other than James Brown, known as the Godfather of Soul. The singer lived near Al's old home in Queens, but he was famous worldwide, especially among African Americans. And Brown wanted to do a benefit concert for the NYM. Al was incredibly excited.

James Brown invited the reverend to one of his concerts in Newark, New Jersey. Sharpton and Ellis Fleming, a businessman and board member of the NYM, went backstage to meet the singer in his dressing room before the show. Al was awestruck, almost speechless—which was quite unusual for the boy preacher! But the singer had been thinking about Al and had some plans for him.

"Young man, I understand you've got a lot of authority, and if you listen to me, you might become the biggest young man in the country," Brown began. As the singer continued talking and asking questions, the reverend just kept nodding and saying, "Yes, Mr. Brown, yes sir."

As Brown headed out of his dressing room, Al and Fleming walked along with him. Suddenly, they came to a place where Brown reached out and grabbed a microphone and started singing. Al Sharpton had just

Singer James Brown (left) walks with Sharpton from the White House in Washington, D.C.

walked onstage with James Brown, in front of thousands of people! He and Fleming looked up in surprise. Then they sort of danced their way off the stage.

The reverend and the singer talked some more after the show and over the next few weeks. Brown said he was doing a show in Brooklyn. He said the show would raise funds for the National Youth Movement if Al would help him advertise it. Brown told him exactly what to do, what ads to put on the radio, and where to put up posters. The tickets sold so well that Brown actually did two shows that night.

LIKE FATHER, LIKE SON

The young reverend did such a good job following James Brown's instructions that the singer invited him to tour the country with him that summer. Al used the opportunity to promote his National Youth Movement. He hoped to set up chapters as far away as Los Angeles, California.

The two became so close they were like father and son. Al, of course, had not seen his real father for some time. He missed him. But being with James Brown reminded him of good times with his dad— like the time they waited in line for hours to see James Brown at the Apollo Theater. Brown's son Teddy, a friend of Al's, had been killed in a car accident, so in a way, the singer could look on Al as another son.

The next year Sharpton and James Brown used a trick to get Brown's show into the vast Madison Square Garden auditorium in New York City. Auditorium officials had refused to let James Brown appear there, complaining that his fans were too rowdy. So the National Youth Movement rented the Garden, then invited James Brown in to play. There was nothing the theater's officials could do about it. Brown sold out the Garden for his July 4, 1974, concert.

The two were still close friends in 1981, when James Brown was invited to the White House to talk to Vice President George H. W. Bush on Martin Luther King Day. Brown decided he wanted Al to go with him. But first, Brown took the reverend to a hairdresser in Georgia and asked her to make Sharpton's hair look like his own—high, swept-back, and shiny. Brown explained that "when we go to the White House there's going to be a lot of press, and when people see him I want them to see me, like he's my son." Sharpton agreed to the hairstyle change. Brown asked him to keep his hair like that as long as Brown was alive. The reverend has done so, even though people who don't know the whole story sometimes make fun of his hair.

Sure enough, at the White House the two men were photographed together—the thin singer and the bulky preacher, with their matching hairstyles. When they met with the vice president, James Brown said he felt things were going wrong in the country. "Tell us what to do, Mr. Brown," the vice president kept saying. Finally Brown pointed to the reverend. "You tell him!" he said. So the reverend had to think of some ideas on the spot.

At another point in the two men's friendship, Brown was appearing in England and Sharpton was with him. Brown's manager had a heart attack and went back to the United States. Brown asked the reverend to fill in. One task the reverend had to do as manager was to hire a new backup singer for Brown. A band member recommended a young lady named Kathy Jordan, from Niagara Falls, New York. Brown agreed, and she was hired. But something else happened: the reverend and the young singer fell in love. (The reverend had been married very briefly once before, to RCA recording artist Marsha Tinsley, whom he had dated in school.) He and Kathy were married in 1980, and they soon had two daughters.

Through James Brown, Sharpton continued to be involved in the music business over the next decade, even as he led the National Youth Movement and preached in churches. He also combined these activities, focusing the NYM on racism in the music business. African American performers were popular with people of all races. But other people in the music business, such as the top concert promoters, were still most often white. So the reverend organized protests against African American singers who used white promoters, demanding they work with African Americans. Among the artists he targeted were Whitney Houston, Marvin Gaye, and the Jackson Five, made up of Michael Jackson and his brothers.

Some of the entertainers Sharpton targeted were willing to listen. Others were not. Marvin Gaye was angry at the protests and never agreed to cooperate. The protests upset Whitney Houston as well, but she met with Sharpton and others and began hiring African American promoters. And when the reverend called for African American involvement in the Jackson Family Victory Tour in 1984, the Jacksons hired him to distribute free tickets and organize security patrols with young people from the cities the tour visited.

Sharpton and his wife, Kathy, renewed their marriage vows in 2001.

Sharpton and other activists were arrested in New York City at a subway station in Harlem.

SEVEN

Howard Beach

In the 1960s, the civil rights movement showed Americans how strong racism was in the South. In states such as Alabama and Mississippi, African Americans were ridiculed and attacked if they tried to exercise their right to vote, to attend quality schools, and to march in protest. Many people in the North liked to think that racism was a southern problem. Certainly, many New Yorkers felt that way. But plenty of incidents revealed racism in the North, sometimes involving police mistreatment of African Americans. However, these events gained nowhere near the attention that problems in the South did.

Working out of the National Youth Movement's donated offices in Brooklyn's St. Mary's Hospital, the reverend would hear of various racist incidents around New York. He often became involved in them. One

Bernhard Goetz and the Law

Did Bernhard Goetz have the right to shoot the four youths if he thought he was being robbed and his own life was in danger? The court that tried him initially decided that Goetz did have that right. But another court corrected that ruling. The higher court said that not only did Goetz have to have feared for his life, but the fear also had to be reasonable. That change became important sixteen years later, when four New York police officers shot an unarmed man named Amadou Diallo. A jury had to decide whether the four officers were reasonably afraid of being shot themselves.

such incident took place on December 22, 1984. While riding on the subway that day, a white man, Bernhard Goetz, was asked by four African American young men for five dollars. The men didn't know it, but Goetz had been robbed before. Now he carried a gun. Goetz stood up, pulled out the gun, and fired off multiple shots, hitting all four of the young men. One was left paralyzed.

News of the "subway vigilante," as Goetz was called, spread quickly. It caused strong reactions among New Yorkers. Some praised Goetz for acting against crime. Many others felt he had overreacted. They said he had pulled a gun and shot young people who had not threatened him at all. Because Goetz was white and the youths were black, many suspected racism, both in the incident itself and in how it was handled by the authorities.

For Sharpton, the Goetz case was deeply disturbing. He felt that many of the young people he worked with could easily have been involved in a situation like that. So he held a press conference on the steps of New York's city hall to speak his views. He also organized prayer vigils and protests outside Goetz's apartment house and later outside the courthouse, too. In the end, Goetz was acquitted in the shooting but convicted of carrying a gun illegally. He was sent to prison for 250 days— just a little more than eight months.

Around this time Sharpton also helped lead a group of protesters at Grand Central Station, New York City's major train station. The protesters were upset that there were too few African Americans on the board and management of the Metropolitan Transit Authority. That's the company that operates the city's buses, subways, and other trains. The reverend and two others sat down on the tracks, delaying trains during rush hour. Eventually the state governor, Mario Cuomo, agreed to appoint an African American to the board.

Mario Cuomo served as governor of New York from 1983 to 1995.

A NEW YORK LYNCHING

Sharpton's activities played a relatively minor role in the Goetz case. In a way, they were a warm-up to what came two years later. Late on December 20, 1986, the phone rang at the reverend's home with a call from one of the kids he worked with at the National Youth Movement. Derrick Jeter was crying on the phone. He kept saying, "They killed my friend out in Queens." The reverend promised he would go to the friend's home in the morning and find out what it was all about.

When Sharpton arrived the next morning he found the friend's mom sitting there with her boyfriend, Cedric Sandiford. Sandiford had cuts and bruises, and his clothing was torn. He'd just gotten in after being questioned by police.

Sandiford told Sharpton what he'd told the police. He and another man, Timothy Grimes, and Derrick's friend Michael Griffith had been in the Queens neighborhood called Howard Beach when their car broke down. He said the three, all African Americans, tried to find a phone to call for help (this was before people had cell phones) when they were taunted by a crowd of white people.

The three went into a pizzeria. When they left, the white group followed them, making clear that African Americans weren't welcome in Howard Beach. A fight broke out and the three men ran. They were chased by the crowd, which Sandiford said was armed with rocks and sticks and even knives. Sandiford and Grimes ran and hid by an expressway. Derrick's friend Michael Griffith tried running onto the expressway to escape. He was hit by a car and killed.

Sandiford also told the reverend that, when the police found him beaten and bleeding, they treated him not as the victim of an attack but as a criminal himself. They did not treat his wounds and were not sympathetic to his story. Instead of asking who had attacked him, they demanded to know why he'd been in Howard Beach.

As Sharpton listened, he became angry. All the racism he'd ever experienced came back to him—from the time his father was turned away from the burger joint in North Carolina to the Bernhard Goetz incident. He told Sandiford and the Griffith family that he and the National Youth Movement would do everything they could to seek justice.

Meanwhile, reporters and camera crews had gathered outside the house. Sharpton told the journalists what he'd learned. He said the death was a racially motivated killing. There were other visitors to the house that day. One was New York City's mayor, Ed Koch. The mayor called Griffith's death a "racial lynching." That compared it to the murders of African Americans by lawless mobs in the South.

Cedric Sandiford (seated, center) speaks at a press conference with his lawyers and Sharpton.

SHARPTON PUSHES FOR JUSTICE

Although the mayor promised the authorities would act, Sharpton didn't trust him. He felt the mayor had been hostile to him in the Goetz case. So the reverend announced that he would hold a rally in front of the Howard Beach pizzeria the next day. He called for people to meet him at the Griffiths' house, and they would drive there together. After making this announcement, he realized that he didn't have a car himself, so he asked a friend who was a labor union leader to drive him.

When he arrived at the Griffiths' the next day there were more than one hundred cars waiting, each filled with people ready to go to Howard Beach. They included his supporters, labor leaders, and other ministers. The group tied a red ribbon on each car's antenna and headed for the neighborhood of the attack.

Despite the tense situation, people got out of their cars at the pizzeria. The reverend made a speech. Then he went into the pizzeria, pulled out a $100 bill, and ordered pizza for everyone who was with him. The man at the counter just kept handing out pizza slices to everyone there.

The next weekend there was an even bigger demonstration in Howard Beach. More than a thousand protesters turned out. So did several hundred angry people on the other side. They taunted the protesters with shouts of "Animal!" and "Go home!" TV crews, reporters, and photographers were there, too, recording the whole thing. Their reports would show that racial hatred was not just a southern problem. Similar scenes had been filmed decades earlier in such places as Selma, Alabama, but not in New York.

A DAY OF OUTRAGE

Meanwhile local authorities were moving to prosecute members of the white mob responsible for the attacks. The district attorney said he would bring criminal charges against those involved. But when he announced the charges at the Queens County Courthouse, he said the mob members would be charged with "reckless endangerment." That's a less serious charge than murder or manslaughter, which might be expected in an incident in which someone is killed.

The families of the three who were attacked were angry. So were their supporters. Their attorneys and Sharpton worked out a strategy: the two survivors of the attack would not help the authorities in any way. Their help was needed by the prosecutors if they were to take the members of the mob to court. Sharpton's job was to keep the pressure up, to make sure New Yorkers didn't forget about the case. He did that by organizing marches and protests. He kept stirring things up every way he could.

This strategy was controversial. Would Sharpton make things worse by keeping reasonable people from being heard? Didn't the victims have a

Sharpton organized several rallies in Howard Beach, Queens, to keep pressure on authorities to continue investigating the attack. Here, Sharpton and other protesters visit New Park Pizza, where the Howard Beach incident began.

BOROUGH HALL

Sharpton (foreground, pointing toward platform), blocked subway tracks during a demonstration against racism that marked the first anniversary of the Howard Beach attacks.

responsibility to work with police and prose-cutors to see justice done? But Sharpton's plan turned out to be effective. The governor of New York State, Mario Cuomo, appointed a special prosecutor to look at new charges in the case. Sharpton and the families didn't trust this man, either, so the reverend kept organizing protests. Then the new prosecutor announced that four members of the white mob would be charged with murder and manslaughter.

It took about a year to get ready for the trial. During this time, Sharpton continued to work on the case and to speak out against racist incidents throughout New York. When the trial began, Sharpton and other activists worked to make sure the courtroom was packed every day.

Finally the time came for the jury to make a decision. Under the American sys-tem, jurors are to be shielded from outside pressures. But Sharpton and the others decided they wanted everyone to know just how important this case was to African Americans and how they viewed racism in the city. They decided to organize a "Day of Outrage."

On December 21, 1987, a year and a day after the attacks at Howard Beach, Sharpton and others went down to the subway station at Brooklyn's Borough Hall. They wanted to hold the doors of a train open. That would stop the train, blocking the tracks and tying up subway traffic. Subway workers knew what they were up to, though. The workers refused to stop any trains at the station.

That didn't slow down the reverend. He'd organized a subway strike once before. He climbed down onto the tracks, carefully avoiding the dangerous, high-voltage rail that powers the subway. So did the people with Sharpton. Other protesters blocked traffic on the Brooklyn Bridge. They stopped other subway cars by jumping onto the tracks, pulling emergency cords, and even dangling their legs over train platforms. "No justice, no peace!" chanted the demonstrators. Many of the hundreds of thousands of people who rode the subways each day were held up for hours by the protest. So were many cars on the Brooklyn Bridge.

Police arrested Sharpton and the people with him on the tracks. But more protesters kept jumping down. Eventually, seventy-three people were jailed. They would stay in jail all night until they could be taken to court the next morning. Meanwhile, the jury was still deliberating in the Howard Beach case.

About five o'clock the next morning, a new shift of jail guards came in. One guard walked up to the reverend's cell. "Hey, Sharpton, you really showed 'em, man," he told the weary protester. "What?" asked the reverend. "The verdict came back," said the guard. "They're guilty." Three of the four defendants were convicted of manslaughter and of assaulting Cedric Sandiford. Only one defendant was acquitted.

Sharpton leaves court after pleading innocent to charges of fraud and larceny. He was later found not guilty.

EIGHT

Protests, Trials— and a Stabbing

After the Howard Beach case it seemed Al Sharpton had an unending stream of racial injustices to challenge. It didn't matter whether the victim was a teen shot by police as he cut through a neighbor's yard or a sixty-six-year-old grandmother killed while holding a butter knife. The reverend and his supporters felt that African American lives just didn't count for much in New York City. It seemed to them that African Americans could be killed or injured by police or racist gangs with no one to speak up for them.

But the reverend was certainly willing to speak up. He did it well, arranging protests and giving press conferences guaranteed to make the evening news. He was so good at this that his critics began calling him the Reverend Soundbite, as if all he wanted was to get on TV. For the families of African Americans killed or injured in incidents that appeared to involve racism, the reverend became the person to call.

One such case began during the Howard Beach trial. In the town of Wappingers Falls, New York, a fifteen-year-old girl had been found in a

Talk show host Phil Donahue (with microphone) moderates a discussion about the Brawley case at the Bethany Baptist Church in Brooklyn.

trash bag with excrement smeared on her body and racist graffiti written on her torso in charcoal. Taken to the hospital, she barely communicated with anyone. A police officer came and tried to talk to her. Using gestures and nodding her head in answer to his questions, the girl seemed to claim she had been assaulted and held by a group of white men that included at least one police officer.

Several law enforcement agencies investigated the case, including the Federal Bureau of Investigation (FBI). They were hampered by the fact that the girl, Tawana Brawley, never gave them a full account of what happened. About a week before the verdict in the Howard Beach case, there was a rally in support of Tawana in a nearby town. The rally was at a church whose pastor, the Reverend Saul Williams, knew Sharpton from his "Wonderboy Preacher" days. Sharpton was one of the speakers at the rally.

A few weeks later, the reverend and the two lawyers he'd worked with in the Howard Beach case—Alton Maddox and C. Vernon Mason—became advisers to the Brawley family. For the reverend, the girl's claims brought to mind every outrage suffered by the African American women he knew, including the challenges his own mother had faced.

The three advisers worked to keep the Brawley case in the public eye, even as they tried to stop investigators from talking to the girl and her mother, Glenda Brawley. At one point, Glenda was called to testify before a grand jury. Sharpton felt she should not testify until suspects were in custody, so he arranged for her to take refuge in an African American church. TV talk show host Phil Donahue came to the church basement where Glenda was staying and broadcast a TV show with Sharpton from there. The reverend himself became a big part of the story—and a target for attacks. TV stations ran reports claiming that the Reverend Sharpton secretly knew the case was a hoax or had hired detectives to plant listening devices. Another report accused him of having been an FBI informant.

In the end, no one was ever charged in the Tawana Brawley case. Brawley's supporters believe justice was impossible because the police and other investigators were out to protect their colleagues. Brawley's critics claim that, with the help of Sharpton and the other advisers, Tawana and her family avoided having to give information about what happened. They say that, if investigators had gotten a full account from the girl, they would have found that part or all of it was untrue.

Eventually, the case did spark at least one trial. But it was Tawana's three advisers who were on trial. During their campaign on her behalf, they accused a local prosecutor of being one of the girl's attackers. A grand jury investigated and said there was no way the prosecutor could have been involved. Later the prosecutor sued the three men for making false

Grand Juries

Under the U.S. legal system, prosecutors cannot just decide to charge someone with a serious crime. They must first convince a group of ordinary people, called a grand jury, that there is evidence to back up the charges. Grand juries meet in secret in order to protect people. But the secrecy, and the fact that prosecutors often control what evidence is heard, leads some people to question whether grand juries really provide protection against injustice.

claims about him. He won, and the reverend was ordered to pay the prosecutor $65,000.

The Brawley case, which received attention all over the country, fixed a clear opinion of the Reverend Al Sharpton in many people's minds. To some, he was nothing but a flamboyant self-promoter, interested only in seeking the maximum amount of publicity for himself. To others, he was a shining knight in a pompadour hairdo, always ready to come to the support of African Americans in trouble.

THE REVEREND ON TRIAL

One day, the reverend got a call from James Brown. Though the two no longer worked together, they were still close. The singer would sometimes call the reverend and jokingly make sure that Sharpton still had his James Brown–style hairdo. In 1988, Brown was arrested in South Carolina after a car chase and was jailed for three years on various charges. He called the reverend regularly from jail.

This time, though, Brown called and asked the reverend to guess where he was. "In jail in South Carolina?" asked Sharpton.

Tawana Brawley is flanked by attorney Alton Maddox (left) and Sharpton as she faces the media to deny reports that she lied about her alleged kidnapping and assault.

No, Brown said, he was in Albany, New York's state capital, where he was being asked to testify against Sharpton in front of a grand jury investigating the reverend himself.

From this and other tips, Sharpton learned that he was being investigated by state prosecutors. He believed the New York attorney general, the state's top legal officer, was out to get revenge on him for his activities in the Brawley case. The attorney general had been appointed by the governor as special prosecutor in that case.

Sure enough, in 1990 Sharpton was indicted, or charged by the grand jury, on sixty-seven charges. It was claimed that he'd stolen money from the National Youth Movement and also failed to report it on his income taxes. The reverend was at home when he first heard of this. His phone rang, and the police said they had surrounded his house and were going to arrest him. They may have been worried that, because he was so popular, he might be difficult to arrest. But the reverend just pulled a jacket on over his jogging suit, which was his preferred clothing at the time, and went out to be taken to court.

Sharpton was arrested at New York's LaGuardia Airport during a demonstration protesting the city's handling of racial incidents.

The police officers who arrested him walked him in front of a long line of TV cameras, photographers, and reporters at the courthouse. That was what they did when they'd caught a villain they were particularly proud of catching.

The reverend had known this was coming. He decided that being arrested like this meant that he'd really arrived. After all, hadn't it happened to his heroes, from Marcus Garvey to Adam Clayton Powell? So he tried to let everyone know he didn't take the matter too seriously. In court, when a judge asked how Sharpton pleaded, his attorney would normally have answered for him: "Not guilty, your honor." But the reverend spoke up first. "I plead the attorney general insane!" he blurted out. That smart remark made everybody laugh.

After the hearing he was taken out past all the cameras again. At this point, many people charged with crimes try to hide their faces. Not the reverend. "They did this to King! They did this to Powell! They did this to Garvey! This is my inauguration! I have arrived!" he shouted. The next day, the headline in one of New York City's newspapers read: "SHARPTON INDICTED ON FRAUD, GRAND LARCENY AND TAX RAPS. RETORTS: 'I THINK THE ATTORNEY GENERAL IS INSANE.'"

During his trial prosecutors called more than eighty witnesses, many of them people who had worked closely with Sharpton. Over two months they tried to prove he had stolen about $250,000 from the National Youth Movement. Finally, the last prosecution witness was called.

Then it was time for Sharpton and his lawyer to call their own witnesses and show their own evidence. But the lawyer, Alton Maddox, decided to try a risky strategy. He knew that, in the United States, courts work under what is called "the presumption of innocence." That means

that—in theory, at least—defendants never have to prove they're innocent. Instead, prosecutors must prove a defendant guilty. Maddox didn't
think the prosecutors had done that. So he called not a single witness in
Sharpton's defense. "The defense rests, your honor," he said.

It was a very risky move, but it was a successful one. Less than six
hours later, the jurors said they'd reached a verdict of "not guilty" on
every one of the sixty-seven charges. The verdict was a huge rebuke to
the prosecutors who had brought the reverend into court.

Sharpton still had to face three more charges in Albany for failing to
file his state income tax forms. But with the failure of the big case in
New York City, there was no way those charges could stick. The government and the reverend agreed that the tax case could be settled if
Sharpton agreed to pay a fine.

A KNIFE IN BENSONHURST

It was early morning on August 23, 1989, when, as had happened so
many times before, the reverend's phone rang with a call for help. A
group of African American youths had gone into the Brooklyn neighborhood of Bensonhurst shopping for a used car. It was a dangerous
place for young black men. Soon they were attacked, and one of them,
sixteen-year-old Yusuf K. Hawkins, was shot twice through the heart.
That morning, as the reverend was calling around and checking into the
incident, Yusuf Hawkins's father called him.

The New York authorities immediately responded to the shooting
in a strong way. They'd learned not to ignore a racially motivated killing.
Still, the reverend began leading protests. People in Bensonhurst

responded by throwing things at the protesters and shouting things like "Send 'em back to Africa." Some of those responsible for the murder were charged and convicted. But by the next year the reverend was worried that the prosecutors were slowing down. They were not moving forward against others who had also been involved in the murder.

As he'd done many times before, Sharpton called for a protest march in Bensonhurst. He decided to hold it the weekend before Martin Luther King's birthday in 1991. It would be the twenty-ninth march he had organized there since Yusuf Hawkins was killed. By now, the police knew to set aside a schoolyard where the protesters could meet and get organized before marching.

Sharpton got out of his car and was walking toward the protesters when he thought he felt someone punch him in the chest, hard. He saw a white man, with a real look of hate on his face. Then the reverend looked down and saw a knife handle sticking out of his own chest. "I've been stabbed!" he thought. He grabbed the knife by the handle and pulled it out. Then he fell to his knees, his hands bloody, and some of the people around him started screaming.

Sharpton and two of the beating survivors participate in an anti-racism march through the largely white Bensonhurst section of Brooklyn, where Yusuf Hawkins was killed.

Sharpton held a press conference in the hospital while he was recovering from a stab wound near his heart.

One of Sharpton's assistants who had been a professional football player, along with one of his guards and Yusuf Hawkins's dad, chased and tackled the reverend's attacker. They held him until police arrested the man.

Sharpton was rushed to the hospital. When he realized the doctors were cutting away his clothing to treat his wound, he stood up and took off his long leather jacket. He didn't want his new jacket damaged. The doctors found the stab wound was more than three inches deep, and the knife had come close to his heart. They operated on him to repair his injury.

When Sharpton woke up after surgery there was a group of men in hospital masks standing over him. One kept saying, "Call for peace. Al, call for peace." It was David Dinkins, the reverend's lawyer from the 1970s who was now mayor of New York. As soon as Sharpton answered that of course he wanted peace, Dinkins rushed outside and told reporters and TV crews that Al Sharpton was calling for peace. The mayor had been worried that the city might erupt in violence after the attack.

Other people came in, including the reverend's wife, Kathy. She worked for the Army Reserve and had been at an army base near Bensonhurst the day of the stabbing. After all the visitors had left, Sharpton called Jesse Jackson. The two men had become divided over some issues. But Sharpton realized that Jackson was the one minister in the civil rights movement he really looked to as an example. They talked, and Jackson flew to New York the next day to visit.

There were lots of calls and visitors while he was in the hospital, but one call stood out. A nurse handed Kathy Sharpton a note saying that a man from Orlando, Florida, had called. The man claimed to be the reverend's dad. He said he'd seen the stabbing on TV and wanted to talk to his son. There were many things the reverend had wanted to say to his dad over the years: "Where were you when I was graduating, when I was on trial, when I was thinking of dropping out of college? Where were you when I needed you?" But none of that seemed to matter. The reverend just called his dad back and talked to him for the first time in years.

Three years later, Sharpton's father and half-sister Ernestine attended the wedding of his sister, Cheryl. The reverend himself performed the ceremony. It was a family reunion of sorts, the first time everyone had been together in twenty-nine years.

In 1992, Sharpton's attacker was sentenced for the stabbing. The reverend showed up to ask the judge for leniency—that is, to go easy on the sentencing. Thirteen years later, the city agreed to pay the reverend $200,000 to settle his claims that the police officers present at the incident carelessly failed to protect him.

Sharpton first decided to run for office in 1992 with the hopes of highlighting the lack of African Americans in state and federal government.

NINE

Into Politics

Al Sharpton went home from the hospital after just a week, but full recovery took much longer. At first he simply had to stay in bed. He did this in the family's new apartment in New Jersey, where he and Kathy had moved with their daughters, Dominique and Ashley. For the annual march over the Brooklyn Bridge in honor of Dr. King on January 21, the reverend took the route in a wheelchair.

When Sharpton was well enough to travel, Jesse Jackson invited him and Kathy out to Las Vegas for a birthday party for his wife, Jacqueline. The two couples spent five days together, and the two men were able to sit down and talk at length.

The stabbing and the talks with Jackson caused Sharpton to think over where he'd been heading in life. For several years, he and Alton

Maddox had been leading a group called the United African Movement in rallies at a place called the Slave Theater in Brooklyn. After his recovery, the reverend was welcomed back to the rallies. But he was also challenged by militants—activists who believed in taking aggressive action. They wanted to know why he'd been photographed with people such as Mayor Dinkins and Jesse Jackson after the stabbing. The militants believed that these men were too willing to compromise in the fight against racism. They wanted nothing to do with the likes of Dinkins and Jackson. They wanted the reverend to have nothing to do with them as well.

For Sharpton, the militant approach did not feel quite right. The man who had stabbed him had acted out of pure hatred—the reverend had seen it on his face. But it would be wrong to return the hatred. Didn't the Bible say it was wrong to return hatred for hatred? A famous Princeton University professor, Cornel West, later told him that "you come out of Martin's house, not Malcolm's." What West meant was that Sharpton came from the nonviolent tradition of Martin Luther King Jr., not the more militant tradition of the African American leader Malcolm X.

Of course, Sharpton was still involved in challenging racism. One major incident took place in Crown Heights in 1991, where Sharpton had once lived. The Brooklyn neighborhood was divided between African Americans and Hasidic Jews, who wear distinctive clothes and are carefully observant of their religious laws. Both African Americans and Jews had been the targets of racism. Both often cooperated in the civil rights movement. But relations between the two groups in Crown Heights were hostile.

Things came to a head when a car driven by a Hasidic Jew went out of control at an intersection and struck and killed a seven-year-old African

American boy, Gavin Cato. It also injured his cousin Angela. The driver of the vehicle was attacked by angry African Americans at the scene. Injured in the attack, he was taken away by ambulance before the injured girl was. Word of the incident spread. So did the violence. Yankel Rosenbaum, a young Jewish man studying to be a rabbi, or Jewish religious leader, was attacked by a mob of African Americans and stabbed to death.

With two tragic deaths and continued rioting, tensions were high. Gavin Cato's family called in Sharpton. He worked with them, helping

Racial violence broke out in the Crown Heights section of Brooklyn in 1991.

with funeral arrangements and other things. He also organized a march to the cemetery where Gavin was to be buried. It was the first nonviolent event of the week. Mayor Dinkins wanted Sharpton to help calm the situation, and the reverend wanted to help. But he was also concerned because he believed the police were arresting mainly African American youths as the disturbances continued. Sharpton told the mayor he would have to release those youths.

Eventually a grand jury refused to indict the driver who had struck and killed Gavin Cato. And the young black man accused of killing Yankel Rosenbaum was acquitted. After that acquittal, people sympathetic to Rosenbaum tried tactics that could have been copied from the reverend himself—marching and calling for further investigations.

A TRY FOR THE SENATE

By 1992 Sharpton was turning from protests and marches to another means to get his message across. In 1984 and 1988, the Reverend Jesse

Minorities in the Senate

There are one hundred U.S. senators—two per state. At the time Al Sharpton decided to run, only three African Americans had ever served in the Senate. Two of those had served more than a hundred years before. Sharpton wasn't elected in 1992, but Carol Mosely-Braun, an African American woman from Illinois, was. She became one of five new women senators elected in 1992.

Jackson had run for president of the United States. There hadn't been much chance that Jackson would actually win. He was an activist who had never held office and was not a politician. But people running for president have a tremendous opportunity to speak and have their voices heard. They can raise whatever issues they think are important. Their words are reported on TV and in the newspapers. The other candidates running against them have to respond. Jackson's two runs for president helped put African American concerns and issues in the spotlight.

Sharpton decided he could do the same thing in New York. He would run for the U.S. Senate. Simply by declaring that he was running, he could remind people there were no African Americans at all serving in the Senate. No African American had ever been elected to a statewide office in New York, either.

Sharpton entered the Senate race on Martin Luther King Day, January 20, 1992. He opened his campaign

Sharpton shakes hands with Geraldine Ferraro after a debate among the Democrats vying to become one of New York's senators.

office on Adam Clayton Powell Boulevard in Harlem. At first, many people thought his candidacy was a joke. In fact, many people thought the reverend himself was a joke, with his funny hair and a speaking style that seemed more quick than thoughtful.

Sharpton would be running as a Democrat. First, he needed to win the primary race. The winners of the Democratic and Republican primaries would then face off in the general election. Leaders of the Democratic Party tried to keep Sharpton out of the race at first. But then they changed their minds. And that decision proved to be a good one when the reverend gave a powerful speech at the state party convention. He won a standing ovation from the delegates. The *New York Times* ran a story calling Sharpton "a candidate who has surprised a lot of people."

The other candidates used expensive advertising in their campaigns. But the reverend's low-budget campaign relied on his speaking to crowds and meeting people. He was already an expert at this. The

Though Sharpton finished third in the primary, his campaign helped publicize issues that he felt were ignored by mainstream politicians.

"Wonderboy Preacher" had never stopped preaching. Now he just increased that activity, visiting five or six churches every Sunday. He came not as a stranger but as someone who had often been there before. In many ways, Sharpton felt like he'd been preparing for this campaign his whole life.

As he campaigned, he talked about problems with jobs, housing, and the criminal justice system. He wanted a special prosecutor to handle cases where there might have been racial violence or abuses by the police. He also wanted more African Americans in the criminal justice system, from police to prosecutors to judges.

During the campaign he often stayed in the housing projects. It was a good way to campaign. He'd meet the neighbors and meet with the tenants' association. In the morning, he would go out to shake people's hands as they got on the subway.

When the votes were counted in September 1992, the reverend, as expected, did not win. But he did place third among the four candidates in the Democratic primary. That put him ahead of a top city official whom everyone had considered a more "serious" candidate. In all, the reverend won more than 161,000 votes statewide. That was 15 percent of the total votes cast in the four-way race. He did even better in New York City, winning 21 percent of the vote. "The real winner tonight is Al Sharpton," one politician said after the votes were counted.

Sharpton had run unsuccessfully for U.S. Senate and mayor for more than a decade before he announced his candidacy for president.

TEN

Candidate Sharpton

The reverend was standing where he was most comfortable: in the pulpit of a church. True, it was a Baptist church in South Carolina, not a familiar church in New York. But he wasn't there because Carpentersville Baptist Church wanted to bring in a good preacher that Sunday. Al Sharpton was there because he was running for president. For months now, he'd been preaching in churches all over South Carolina.

"We have gone from property to president," Sharpton told the congregation that day in February 2004. "No one would have ever thought back in the days when we were stood up and sold as chattel that one of us would one day be running for the presidency." He was referring to the days African Americans were sold as slaves.

More than a decade had passed since the reverend's first run for the Senate in New York. He tried for Senate again two years later and then for mayor in 1997. He did not win in any of those elections, although he got almost one-third of the votes in the mayoral primary. Some people attacked him for these campaigns. Because he'd proven he could get

Sharpton wasn't discouraged by his losses and instead continued campaigning.

thousands of votes, they said, why didn't he run for an office he was likely to win? Because New York sends several congresspeople to the U.S. House of Representatives, he would have a better chance of winning one of those seats.

But the reverend was running for president, just as Jesse Jackson had already done twice. If he'd been unlikely to be elected senator, becoming president was even more unlikely. Even Jackson endorsed a different candidate.

But in his sermon at Carpentersville Baptist Church that day, the reverend was admitting no disadvantage. "There are seven people running," he said. "And I'll tell y'all a secret. Six of them won't win. . . . Don't waste your vote trying to guess who will win. Use your vote to help win who ought to win." By the time the reverend was done with the sermon, all the people in the packed little church were on their feet, shouting and clapping. The church's pastor asked his congregation to pray for the reverend. The pastor also took up a collection so people could donate to the Sharpton campaign.

STILL PROTESTING

The race for president was the reverend's fourth run for office. During all the campaigns, he'd never stopped being an advocate for African Americans and others in trouble. In the midst of his run for the presidency, an African American woman died in Harlem after police raided her apartment by mistake. For any other candidate, it would have been a minor local issue. But for the reverend, it was a call to action as he worked to publicize her death.

Civil Disobedience

When the Reverend Sharpton led people to block the subways or trespass on a military base, he was using a strategy called civil disobedience. Civil disobedience involves breaking the law to show opposition to government policies. It was first written about by the nineteeth-century American writer Henry David Thoreau. Thoreau went to jail rather than pay taxes he believed were used for war. The practice was also used by Mahatma Gandhi, in seeking independence for India, and by Martin Luther King Jr., in seeking civil rights in the United States.

Then in February 1999, a young man from Africa living in New York was shot and killed by four police officers. They said they thought they saw him reaching for a gun. It turned out that the man, Amadou Bailo Diallo, was only reaching for his wallet. The reverend called the usual protests and actions to make sure the death was investigated. What happened next showed both the strengths and weaknesses of Sharpton's approach. The four police officers were indeed charged with murder. But when Sharpton kept up the pressure and continued to organize protests, their trial was moved to another city to make sure they got an unbiased jury. Eventually, the officers were acquitted. That led Diallo's mother to say the reverend may have actually hurt the case by continuing to protest after the four were charged.

More than 1,700 people were arrested during protests over the Diallo case. But Sharpton's longest time in jail came in 2001. He had traveled to Puerto Rico to support people who were upset that the U.S.

military was using a small island there for bombing practice. He and others went onto the military base and were arrested for trespassing. The reverend was shocked at how long his sentence was: eighty-seven days! He spent the time in prison rereading books on such leaders as Martin Luther King, Nelson Mandela of South Africa, and Mahatma Gandhi of India. Every one of them had spent at least some time in jail, often as a result of civil disobedience, the kind of nonviolent protests the reverend often organized. Mandela, who later became president of South Africa, was imprisoned for twenty-seven years. Sharpton said that made his own sentence "look like a trip to Disney World."

Along with the trip to Puerto Rico, Sharpton traveled to other places as well. He went to Africa, where he investigated slavery in the Sudan, to the Middle East to meet with Palestinian leader Yasser

Sharpton shakes hands with Palestinian leader Yasser Arafat during a visit to Israel and the Palestinian territories.

Arafat, and to Cuba to meet with President Fidel Castro. These meetings offended some people. Castro, for instance, held onto power partly by locking up anyone in his own country who caused trouble the way Sharpton did.

Sharpton had been out of jail less than a week when he announced he was thinking of running for president. As a candidate, he decided he would propose three amendments, or changes, to the U.S. Constitution. One would guarantee health care to all Americans. Another would guarantee the right to an education. And the third would guarantee Americans the right to vote. That last proposal seemed a curious one. Don't Americans already have a right to vote? But as the reverend kept pointing out, that right isn't spelled out in the Constitution. Instead, when it comes to electing a president and vice president, the Constitution only talks about voting by "electors" chosen by each state legislature. That removes the elections of the president and vice president from the direct control of the nation's voters.

Its absence had been a factor in the 2000 presidential election, when Al Gore received a half million more votes than George W. Bush, but lost the electoral college vote.

As the race progressed South Carolina became a key state for Sharpton. He was running as a Democrat, and almost half the Democratic voters in the state were African American. The other candidates were out to win African American votes, too. They also spoke in churches. But none seemed to receive the warm welcome given the reverend. He'd been preaching in churches there since the 1960s, and he made about thirty visits to the state before it held its primary election.

That still wasn't enough for Sharpton to win in South Carolina, though. He came in third, far behind the winner, Senator John Edwards, who had been born in South Carolina.

Sharpton may not have won the presidency, but he made a mark that few people expected. During the presidential race, many people expected a Reverend Sharpton who was a radical or a clown, a person no one would take seriously. Instead, when they watched the presidential debates, they saw a man who was intelligent and quick. He was also willing to take on serious issues in ways that the other candidates were afraid to try. One newspaper said the other candidates were worried the reverend would make them all look like accountants, because their words were often bland compared to his.

What would Sharpton do after the election? Pretty much what he'd always done—speak out on behalf of people who'd been wronged and say

Presidential Debates

One of the best ways for voters to compare candidates is through presidential debates. These events force candidates to try to make their points, or show problems with their opponents' ideas, in a forum where they can't control what happens. The biggest change in American presidential debates came when television let viewers across the nation watch. Before TV, only those present in the debate hall could see a debate. The first televised debates in the United States were in 1960, between Richard Nixon and John F. Kennedy. Presidential debates did not appear on TV again until 1976, and they have been televised in every campaign since then.

Throughout his political career, Sharpton has continued to preach.

things that might make others angry but could also make them think.

There was another piece of sad news after the election: Al and Kathy Sharpton announced they'd decided to separate after twenty-four years of marriage. Kathy's absence had already been noticed at official events the reverend attended. He explained to a reporter that she was going back to work in the entertainment industry. "She runs on her track and I run on mine. That's what we promised each other when our kids got older," he told a newspaper reporter. At the time their two daughters, Dominique and Ashley, were eighteen and seventeen.

But the reverend continued to preach. Through all his journeys, Sharpton never gave up his first calling, the one he'd started at age four in Bishop F. D. Washington's church. He's good at it. He reminds people of the troubles they've come through and talks about how he's kept on despite his own troubles. He can talk about the famous people he's known and worked with, such as Martin Luther King Jr., or the everyday people he's met. It's a rare Sunday that the reverend doesn't get the congregation standing and swaying and clapping by the time he's finished, often singing the last part of his sermons.

The Reverend Al Sharpton says the place he loves most in all the world is standing behind a pulpit on a Sunday morning talking about faith and overcoming the odds. "God will make a way for you," he tells people. He sometimes jokes that, if God told him he would die tomorrow at noon, but that he could do whatever he wanted from 11:30 to noon, "I would ask for a church of about three hundred people and preach my way into the hereafter."

Sharpton has always been comfortable at the pulpit, inspiring many with his passion.

Timeline

AL SHARPTON'S LIFE   WORLD EVENTS

1954 Alfred Charles Sharpton Jr. is born on October 3 in Brooklyn, New York, the son of Alfred Charles Sharpton Sr. and Ada Richards Sharpton.

In *Brown v. Board of Education*, the U.S. Supreme Court rules that "separate but equal" schools for African Americans are unlawful.

1957 The Sharpton family joins the Washington Temple Church of God in Christ.

1959 Four-year-old Al preaches his first sermon at the Washington Temple on July 9.

Alaska becomes the 49th U.S. state, and Hawaii becomes the 50th state.

1963 Al Sr. attends the historic March on Washington on August 28.

1964 Ordained at age ten, Al is now the Reverend Alfred Sharpton Jr. and becomes junior pastor of the Washington Temple.

Congress passes the Civil Rights Act.

1964–1973 The United States is involved in the Vietnam War.

1965 Al preaches at the New York World's Fair, appearing with singer Mahalia Jackson.

1967 Jesse Jackson takes over Operation Breadbasket.

1968 Dr. Martin Luther King Jr. is assassinated on April 4.

1969 Al is appointed youth director of Operation Breadbasket.

U.S. astronauts are the first humans to land on the Moon.

1971 Al joins in protests at A & P headquarters in New York City.

The 26th Amendment to the U.S. Constitution lowers the voting age from 21 to 18.

1972 Al graduates from Tilden High School. He holds a luncheon at the New York Hilton to cover the costs of incorporating the National Youth Movement, his own organization.

1973 Sharpton meets soul singer James Brown.

1974 President Richard Nixon resigns in the midst of the Watergate scandal. Vice President Gerald Ford becomes president.

1975 Sharpton drops out of Brooklyn College.

1980 Sharpton weds Kathy Jordan.

1981 Along with James Brown, Sharpton meets Vice President George H. W. Bush at the White House.

1983 Sharpton leads a protest that blocks New York subway trains.

1984 Sharpton protests the Jackson Family's Victory Tour. Jesse Jackson runs for president. Bernhard Goetz shoots four youths on a New York subway on December 22.

1986 The space shuttle *Challenger* explodes after liftoff on January 28.

Michael Griffith is chased onto the freeway and dies in Howard Beach on December 20. Sharpton organizes protests.

1987 The Tawana Brawley case begins.

"Day of Outrage" protests halt commuter traffic on December 21.

1989 Yusuf Hawkins is murdered by a white mob in Bensonhurst on August 23.

The Berlin Wall is torn down, and Eastern Europe is freed from communist rule.

1990 Sharpton is tried and acquitted on sixty-seven charges of stealing from the National Youth Movement.

1991 Sharpton is stabbed while preparing to lead a protest march in Bensonhurst on January 12.

Seven-year-old Gavin Cato is killed by a car in Crown Heights on August 19.

U.S. and allied troops fight the Persian Gulf War in Iraq.

The Soviet Union breaks up into several separate states.

1992 Sharpton runs for the U.S. Senate, winning more than 161,000 votes but placing third out of four candidates in the primary.

1994 Sharpton runs unsuccessfully for the Senate again.

1997 Sharpton runs unsuccessfully for mayor of New York. He wins 32 percent of the vote in the primary.

1999 Amadou Diallo, though unarmed, is shot by New York City police officers on February 4.

2001 Terrorists hijack U.S. airplanes on September 11 and crash them into the World Trade Center in New York City and the Pentagon in Arlington, Virginia.

2003 U.S. troops and their allies invade Iraq.

2004 Sharpton runs unsuccessfully for president of the United States.

To Find Out More

BOOKS

Levine, Ellen. *Freedom's Children:Young Civil Rights Activists Tell Their Own Stories.* New York: Putnam Publishing Group, 2000.

Morrison, Toni. *Remember: The Journey to School Integration.* New York: Houghton Mifflin, 2004.

Steffens, Bradley, and Dan Woog. *Jesse Jackson.* People in the News. Farmington Hills, Mich.: Greenhaven Press, 2000.

Turck, Mary. *The Civil Rights Movement for Kids: A History with 21 Activities.* Chicago: Chicago Review Press, 2000.

DVDS

BET Journeys in Black: Al Sharpton. Black Entertainment Television, 2001.

ORGANIZATIONS AND ONLINE SITES

Al Sharpton on the Issues
http://www.issues2000.org/Al_Sharpton.htm

This Web site shows Al Sharpton's positions on a number of issues when he ran for president in 2004.

The History Makers
http://www.thehistorymakers.com/biography/biography.asp?bioindex=171&category=civicMakers

This is a short biography of Al Sharpton, with links to biographies of many other African American leaders.

National Action Network
http://www.nationalactionnetworklv.org

This Web site of the Las Vegas chapter of the National Action Network, the Reverend Al Sharpton's current organization, provides some history and information about the group.

A Note on Sources

By the mid-1980s, the Reverend Al Sharpton was often in the news. Both stories and photos appearing in the *New York Times*, the *Washington Post*, and the *Chicago Tribune* provided many of the facts from that point forward in the story. Also helpful was a DVD on the reverend produced by BET in 2001. Titled *BET Journeys in Black: Al Sharpton*, the video includes footage of many incidents and interviews with key people.

— *Jay Mallin*

Index

About the Author

Jay Mallin is a journalist, both a writer and a photographer, living in Washington, D.C. His written work has appeared in a number of publications, and his photography has appeared in newspapers and magazines both nationally and internationally. He first heard the Reverend Al Sharpton speak during a Democratic political candidates' forum he was photographing for the forum's organizers in Chicago. Like many people first introduced to the reverend through the 2004 campaign, Jay found that the candidate was quick witted, well spoken, and had an engaging, self-deprecating sense of humor.